The Four Methods of Journal Writing:

Self-Transformation through Memoir

A Spiritual Practice and Ritual for the Soul

by Melissa Burch

Published by **New Memoir Press**

© 2012, Melissa Burch

For more journaling methods, tips, and

information about upcoming events,

please visit and sign up for our newsletter at
www.new-memoir/journalwriting

New Memoir Press
175 Harvey Street, #13
Cambridge, MA 02140
617-491-3374
Melissa@NewMemoirPress.gmail.com

Some names have been changed to protect the identities of individuals in this book.

Dedicated to
Oprah, Martha Beck and Barbara Sher,
whose teachings changed my life, and
to George, Alex and Susana, who walk
this earthly path with me in love.

Table of Contents

INTRODUCTION

Life is a process of becoming, a combination of states we have to go through. Where people fail is that they wish to elect a state and remain in it. This is a kind of death.

— Anaïs Nin

Journal writing touches our deepest core and links us to Spirit, expanding the possibilities of connecting to the Oneness all around us. The practice of writing daily, using *The Four Methods of Journal Writing*, will inspire in you a higher level of consciousness. By following a few simple guidelines, you will unleash a spiritual practice and embrace a ritual honoring the soul.

Journaling is an intimate endeavor, which connects all aspects of the self: the passions, joys, challenges—even the more mundane aspects. That which is hidden, or stuck (e.g. resistance and pain), begins to flow. You find a way out. You see new opportunities. Doors that you hadn't even noticed before open with possibilities. Synchronicity becomes a daily occurrence. "Aha!" moments are integral to your discoveries. Your vitality is so strong that you will not accept what once felt stuck normal and unfulfilling, you can no longer be comfortable with the status quo.

Journal writing takes you across the bridge toward acceptance of your creative self, your spiritual self; accepting what is, with love, joy, and freedom. You will follow my footsteps as a journal writer, one who discovered (at age 50) four methods of journal writing that changed my life.

What I will teach you is based on what I discovered when I took a sabbatical after five years of traveling and teaching homeopathy internationally. During those five years, I wrote six books (some bestsellers in my field), took care of patients in a busy homeopathic practice, hosted a weekly Voice America radio show, and ran the Catalyst School of Homeopathy—all the while taking care of my family, husband, son, and dog.

I was burned out and needed a rest. I felt impelled to review my life, to revisit my memories, and to find answers to life's big questions: "Why am I here?", "What am I meant to be doing?", and "Whom can I serve?".

I began with what I knew for sure: The answers were within me. Journal writing proved to be the most authentic way of finding out what I needed to learn. After half a century on the planet, it was time to understand what brought me to the present, what things gave me pleasure, and what the future might have in store.

Journals from Teenage Years to Present

I want to take you on a journey, to share with you the best methods of journal writing that I have found. It is my hope that you will find yourself writing your own memoir at the end of this adventure.

2

The Four Methods of Journal Writing begins with learning to take time for yourself—maybe in the morning, or before sleep, or whenever you can manage it. As you are creating this new routine you may find that you have different issues at different times. Some methods may resonate more than others. Your specific needs will become clearer as you continue.

I started journal writing in my teen years—when my imagination was endless—when my anger toward my mother, for example, could be expressed with "I hate you!" written across the page. It was the very poetry of adolescence, the uncertainty of growing up.

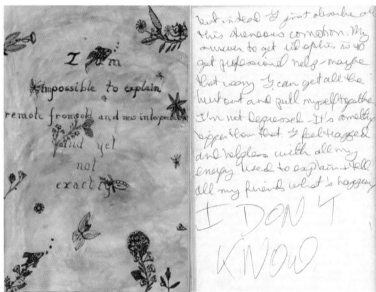
Pages from High School Journal

During my early twenties I wrote about what I wanted in life: to be a filmmaker and a spiritual seeker, have a loving relationship, a job, a home, to travel, etc. Most of the journal entries I wrote during these years read like wish lists…

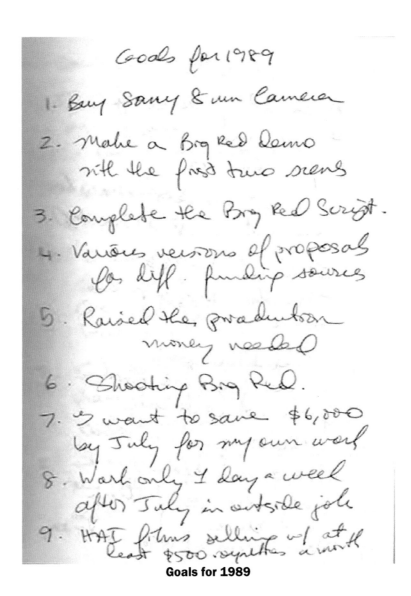

Goals for 1989

...but in my late twenties and early thirties, my journals became more business-oriented and were mostly about plans, goals, contacts, etc...

Business Journal Page

When I was 35, my son was born, and I began an intensive exploration into the self. By this time, I had been meditating daily off and on for ten years. I now started to take my spiritual practices more seriously. I read many books from various spiritual traditions, and joined the Gurdjieff Society, where I attended weekly group meetings. I found that I was ready to see what lay under all my insecurities, anxieties, and self-hatred. The most powerful aid at hand was my journal, which not only helped me heal, but also led, eventually, to self-transformation.

Let us begin the journey.

Method #1: Two-Pages Journaling

The first method I used, **Two-Pages Journaling**, is based on Julia Cameron's "Morning Pages," from her book, *The Artist's Way*. The technique involves setting aside a time every morning to write two pages (Cameron recommends three pages, but I found myself regularly writing two).

Julia Cameron's *The Artist's Way*

The result of this exercise was an outpouring of all my dislikes, morning after morning. Even though my life was full of enchantments (a healthy baby boy, a wonderful husband, and a life that provided many comforts, underneath there was deep dissatisfaction—with self, with others, with circumstances.

Two-Pages Journaling triggered the release of issues that I had pushed down, or tried to fix over and over, not accepting what was, but wanting life to be what I thought it should be. Although the practice was cathartic, this daily spiraling took me deeper and deeper into my unhappiness. So much was lacking; I was just not good enough. (Usually the angst had to do with my feeling fat.)

The writing, self-exploration, and deepening spiritual practice eventually enabled me to accept myself as I was. I didn't need to prove myself to anyone. I could just BE me, with all my flaws and all my attributes. I became someone who believed she had the right to live and contribute to the world.

In Chapter One, **Two-Pages Journaling**, the first method of journal writing, you will find the guidance I myself didn't have through a method that will take you step-by-step to a gentle and profound healing and self-transformation. Like me, you may find that you tap into your dark side through the exercise of writing two pages for five mornings. If that happens, take the work you've done and move it to the next stage. This is where the magic begins.

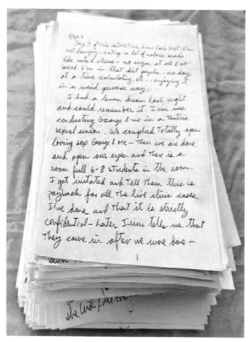

My Two-Pages Journaling Stacked

Method #2: "What Do I Mean by...?" Journaling

In Chapter Two, **"What Do I Mean by...?" Journaling**, will take you much deeper. Here you will search for root causes, patterns, and universality of experiences, which will connect you to Source, a higher consciousness, which will awaken in your life.

"What Do I Mean by…?" Journaling teaches you to observe your bodily sensations while writing. You will sense when something feels charged—a word, an expression, an emotion. As you experience more levels of awareness, you will connect to mysterious and transformative images, thoughts, and feelings that are uniquely your own. Many mystics have sought this awe-inspiring awareness. The overall quality is universal. You are in good company!

"What Do I Mean by…?" Journaling Page

After such a cosmic experience, you may wonder: "What do I do with all this energy and vitality?" Here is where a balance between the inner life and outer life comes together. Your ability to function in the world will improve greatly.

Method #3: Inventions Journaling

In Chapter Three, **Inventions Journaling**, the third method of journal writing, you will track other aspects of your life, following your interests and observations, your desires. You will pay attention to what your mind wants to focus on.

During my sabbatical year I wanted to explore life beyond alternative healing and homeopathy. I had been so focused on healing others, my teaching and advocacy work, that parts of myself had been ignored. This third method of journaling, based on Barbara Sher's book, *Refuse to Choose!*, inspired me to be creative again, to go outside of my comfort zone and test new ideas, to open new channels and see what resonated with me, without the pressure to produce anything, or to succeed.

Barbara Sher's *Refuse to Choose!*

After working with the **Inventions Journaling**, I could map a bigger world from the inside out, trust my instincts, experience synchronicities, navigate new challenges, and set goals for myself that came from my deepest core. It was exciting, refreshing and inspiring.

Inventions Journaling is fun! You will find your creative mind bursting with new ideas. Your challenge will come through integrating these ideas and exploring which of them matter the most to you. You will experience greater harmony between your interior self and the outer world (and with fewer distractions). You will discover the ability to flow with, and navigate, outside circumstances—all important signs of health and well-being.

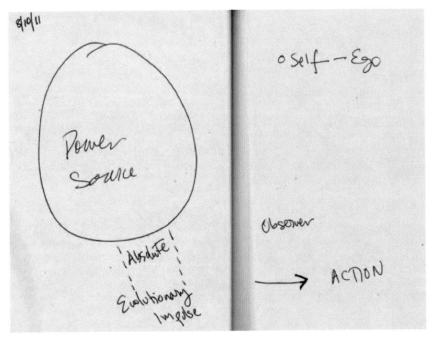

Inventions Journaling Page

As my sabbatical year came to a close (and before my 50th birthday), I had the desire to look back over my five decades and maybe uncover the next step in my life. My friend, Nancy, shared as a birthday gift a method of journaling in which you weave the impressions of your life—the memories, the emotions, the innermost thoughts—in order to find patterns and to see how these imprints can be woven together to guide you forward.

Method #4: Autobiography Journaling

In Chapter Four, Autobiography Journaling, **Method #4: Autobiography Journaling**

In Chapter Four, **Autobiography Journaling**, the fourth method of journaling (based on Nancy's technique), you will have the opportunity to revisit memories and recall significant turning points in your life. The process is validating, helping you to get in touch with who you are and where you came from, so you can leap into what's next for you with a sense of renewed joy and rapture.

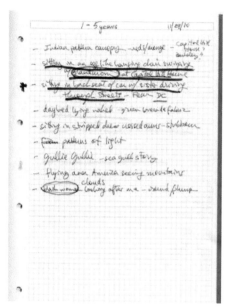

Autobiography Journaling Page

Turning fifty prompted me to re-examine my life. I wondered, "Who am I?", "Why am I here?". I had asked these questions many times before—growing up, reaching middle age, and especially when facing challenges—but now I had a sense of my own mortality, so the questions had greater meaning. I felt I had been offered the chance to understand my many years on this planet, to shape reality from the wisdom of experience, and to pass along to others what I had learned.

These questions, and the **Autobiography Journaling,** led me directly to writing my first memoir, *Face Everything Avoid Nothing: Adventures in War, Filmmaking and Love*, which is about the time I spent as a war journalist in Afghanistan after the Soviet Invasion, when I was in my twenties.

Face Everything Avoid Nothing:

Adventures in War, Filmmaking, and Love

(First Chapter is Available for Free at http://www.new-memoir.com)

After completing *The Four Methods of Journaling*, memoir-writing will be the logical next step. Each day you spend writing your memoir is one of spiritual practice, a ritual for your soul that is noble, courageous, and of benefit to others. Your insights and view of life represent your quintessential self. Your memoir is a celebration of your life—the lessons learned and the gifts to be shared—which goes beyond the self.

The process of writing my memoir forced me to grapple in still greater depth with the bigger questions of life, to learn how to answer these questions for myself, and to translate the answers for others. Each of you has a story to tell. Your life is important, unique and intriguing.

In Chapter 5, **Writing Your Memoir**, I share my experience of this vital work, hoping to inspire you to do the same. Together we will explore taking the personal and making it public. Writing and publishing a memoir represents taking a very public stand. Memoir-writing requires remembering, discovering insights, and connecting to Source—and this creative endeavor will change your life forever. It is time to take yourself seriously.

You start off slow, with **Two-Pages Journaling**, writing each day for the first week (you can continue until the pouring-out feels complete). The flywheel metaphor used in Jim Collin's book, *Good to Great*, is useful here. It fits perfectly with the adventure you are about to begin. As with the flywheel, the momentum builds and you will find yourself coming into contact with Source—a connection where your inner and outer selves meet—and before you know it you will be writing your memoir. I look forward to reading it.

Now let's get started!

CHAPTER 1

Two-Pages Journaling

Anyone who faithfully writes morning pages will be led to a connection with a source of wisdom within.

—Julia Cameron

Preparation for Week 1

Take a look at your schedule and see where you can make available twenty minutes for a period of seven days. This is sacred time with yourself. If you can only find ten minutes a day, then commit to those ten minutes. And if life gets in the way, try not to berate yourself for missing a day. Just start again the next day.

Another possibility would be to schedule twenty minutes during your lunch hour (you may have to tell your office mates that you won't be joining them at the local sandwich shop), or you can plan to go to bed twenty minutes later than usual, and then wake up 20 minutes earlier the next day. Make sure you get enough sleep (8 hours is the bare minimum for most of us). You cannot heal and transform if you are exhausted.

Martha Beck, in her book, *The Four-Day Win: End Your Diet War and Achieve Thinner Peace*, writes about how a habit can be formed over a period of four days. Part of **Two-Pages Journaling** involves making the commitment and getting into the groove of an inner practice that includes writing two pages a day, every day for five days, and completing the **Two-Pages Journaling** in seven days.

Be as flexible as you can with yourself. If you know you have twenty minutes, say, while your child is at daycare on Mondays, then schedule your **Two-Pages Journaling** during that time. On Tuesdays, it could be after your child goes to bed. And so on.

Scheduling Two-Pages Journaling

Tools

You will need a stack of unlined paper. The writing instrument you choose is important. (My favorite is the *Uniball* black pen, which I buy in bulk at Costco). Maybe you prefer a pencil, or a *Montblanc* fountain pen. Find the writing tool that feels right for you.

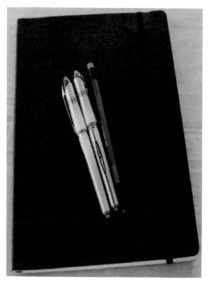

Favorite Journal and Pens

15

If you like, you can make the **Two-Pages Journaling** into more of a ritual. Candles are a special way to honor something important—anniversaries, birthdays, holidays—and they adorn most altars. Tea lights in colored glass containers (with a few drops of lavender essential oil) are an inexpensive option, or you can buy the fancy soya, natural scented candles, or anything in between. It is up to you.

In the first week, find a space where you can light your candle and where there is some privacy (if you can). You are setting off to sail into the unknown. It helps to prepare well for the celebration.

Purpose, Intention, What to Do

The purpose of **Two-Pages Journaling** is to express what is bothering you, what your gripes are, your big issues in life, your fears, your anxieties. This is the time to tell the truth to yourself. If you tend to hide behind a mask of "everything is O.K. with me," remember that this is the time to revisit old wounds, the ones that come to mind spontaneously when you sit down to write your two pages. If you feel like there is more to write, and you have the time, keep going.

This first week is when you examine the dark side. What is not working? Who is upsetting you? Why? What circumstances make you crazy? Be as specific as you can when you write the two pages: name names, write the details. (Be sure to hide your journal if you feel that someone could be hurt by reading what you have written.) Tell where, when, what, how. Write it as if you were talking to your best friend ("She said, he said").

Write fast, or slow. Just follow your pace and don't let that pen off the page. Try not to worry about spelling, penmanship, grammar. Just write—longhand, preferably—don't censor. Write anything that comes to mind, even if it doesn't fit with the instructions I've given you. The key here is to keep writing!

The exercise of **Two-Pages Journaling** will enable you to become more receptive to the subconscious part of yourself, the part that can hide behind emotions, stories, analyzing, distractions, addictions. This takes practice. If you find yourself staring at the page, then write "I'm staring at a blank page." Don't judge yourself. There is no right or wrong here. Just keep the pen on the paper.

Day by day you'll be moving that flywheel. In the beginning it may take more effort, but push hard, make yourself write. What you write can even be gibberish, it doesn't matter. Nobody has to see what you write, only yourself. You can fill the page with one word, if you like. Just do it!

When I work on my **Two-Pages Journaling**, my issues tend to spiral down to "I'm not good enough." This usually starts with my unhappiness about my weight—My clothes don't fit. Either I'm on a diet, or off a diet. Next I might write about some incident which bothered me. My neighbor left trash in the hallways again, for instance. (This pisses me off!) I could write two pages just on that, or maybe even fifteen pages. We all have things that set us off, people who trigger certain feelings in us, something that rubs us the wrong way, something we hoped would happen, that doesn't, etc.

During this week give yourself the space and time to write about the negative side of your life. I know there are schools of thought out there that tell us to always focus on the positive, to set our intentions and visualize what we want. In many ways I agree with these techniques, but they work best when the foundation is strong, when there are no lurking, unresolved issues that have been buried and are liable to resurface at any moment.

Debbie Ford writes, in *The Dark Side of the Light Chasers: Reclaiming Your Power, Creativity, Brilliance and Dreams*, about ways to connect with your dark side so that unresolved issues won't seep out in unproductive ways, sabotaging you, making you reactive, keeping you from forgiving yourself and others, and preventing you from experiencing unconditional love in your life. **Two-Pages Journaling** is a simpler version of taking time to bring to light this dark aspect of yourself, those situations where you feel regret or shame, when you have been hurt by people you love, or just feel stuck in negativity.

For most of you, writing **Two-Pages Journaling** will be cathartic—painful in the moment, perhaps, but afterward you will feel lighter, freer, and more energized. In case a feeling of terror arises in you at the prospect of **Two-Pages Journaling**, however, or if, after the first day, you feel overwhelmed, excessively emotional (weepy, full of rage, vengeful, etc.), or on the verge of catatonic exhaustion, please stop this exercise. Such a severe reaction, while uncommon, may warrant finding a counselor, someone you can trust, to work with you and help you to explore your dark side. It is very important that you do not do this alone. Some of us have deeper wounds than others, and may require extra care. We all need to honor wherever we are in life.

After five days of writing your **Two-Pages Journaling**, it is time to take a break. On Day 6, read over your pages. Remember to breathe and unlock your jaw (move your lower jaw right to left, then left to right) to release any held-in tension. Circle on the page issues that appear repeatedly, themes you notice, strong emotions— anything that stands out. If you have more time, then write down your feelings or any ideas that come to you after reviewing the work you've done so far.

Day 7: It is important to give yourself a day off in between reading your pages to let the unconscious mind percolate. Organize and list the repeated or strong ideas. You can make an outline with sub-categories. Then attach minor issues to the appropriate sub-categories (you can even have a sub-category labeled "Anything else").

Two Pages Journaling Outline

1. Weight issue
   - clothes don't fit
   - hate dieting

2. Financial
   - need to collect unpaid invoices

3. Relationship with Dad
   - new wife

4. Community garbage

5. Anything else:
   - exhausted need to de-clutter closet

Two-Pages Journaling Outline

Another helpful tool is to make a mindmap. Draw a circle in the middle of the page and label it with a date—"My Dark Side, August 22, 2012"—then draw circles (with labels around the middle circle) with the different themes, emotions, situations. Here you can be creative. Use different color pens, draw symbols or pictures, to illustrate your dark side.

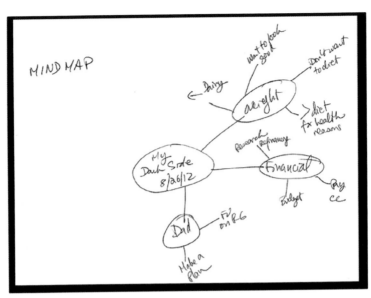

Two-Pages Journaling Mindmap

Last of all, burn your stack of two pages as a ritual letting go, allowing Source to find the best way possible to gently resolve your issues. (Please be conscious of fire safety. A fireplace or outdoor grill are ideal for this purpose. I have used a large, metal stock pot into which I've ripped and burned my pages. You may need to perform this ritual outside, if you have smoke detectors). Be sure to save your outline and/or mindmap for week 2: **"What do I mean by…?" Journaling.**

Review

    1.   Blank paper, a special pen or pencil, and a candle

    2.   Schedule twenty minutes a day for **Two-Pages Journaling** for seven days

    3.   Write Two-Pages during Days 1 – 5

    4.   Day 6: Read what you have written and circle anything that stands out (e.g. repeated, strong emotion[s], etc.)

5.   Write an outline or mindmap of the discoveries you have made from **Two-Pages Journaling**

6.   Burn, in a safe manner, your stack of pages. Save the outline and/or mindmap

CHAPTER 2

"What Do I Mean by...?" Journaling

These ancient teachers maintained that we are communicating with everything, and everything is communicating with us, all the time.

— Martha Beck

Finding Your Way in a Wild New World Any sufficiently advanced technology is indistinguishable from magic.

— Arthur Clarke

Preparation for Week 2

(Or whenever you are ready to move to Journal Writing Method 2)

Now you will need more time, if possible. It is best if you can schedule thirty minutes a day for seven days. Sometimes the freeing of stuck emotions can give you insights into how to solve a problem, which may free up time for you. Maybe you are feeling more energized, and can now be more efficient with daily chores, such as grocery shopping, cooking, cleaning, etc. Setting the intention and making the time a first priority is usually the best approach.

Stephen Covey, in *The 7 Habits of Highly Effective People*, offers the analogy of imagining your most important tasks as large rocks, and all the minor activities, chores, etc., as small pebbles. When you put the small pebbles in first, there is usually not enough room for the larger rocks (major projects). When you put the large rocks, like healing and self-development (or journal writing) in first, then you can add the small pebbles (tasks), and everything will fit nicely in the jar.

Stephen Covey's Visual of Two Jars of Rocks
Photo credit: The Couch Surfing CEO in an excellent post,
"How To Stop Feeling Overwhelmed and Get Your Stuff Done"
by Bradley Gauthier

Sacred Space

Let's slowly create more time, gather our tools, and prepare a sacred space for the second method of journal writing, **"What Do I Mean by...?" Journaling.** Here is where you can add more elements to your journal writing practice.

First, you will need to find a private space for yourself. As Virginia Woolf writes in *A Room of One's Own,* it is important to have one's own personal space. (This is especially true for women. We so often share everything we have with our loved ones.) The martyr in us can sacrifice to the point that sometimes we are self-righteous, overbearing, and demanding. Setting boundaries and making time for yourself is like telling the world that if you are well cared for, everyone around you will be, too. It is healthful to step back and take care of yourself in ways that will, in the long run, serve everyone.

Creating a sacred space is a way of anchoring your energies deeply and profoundly. During the first week of **Two-Pages Journaling**, you started by lighting a candle before writing in order to honor the importance of journal writing in your life. Now I'm asking you to set a stage, an altar, where you can bring powerful symbols (objects) into your consciousness. In this way you can engage with the four elements: water, fire, earth and air. These are ancient themes, which connect you to morphic fields, fields that bring you closer to Oneness, to Source, to the power of the universe.

The candle symbolizes fire in the East, as well as Spirit and illumination, bringing forth the light from within yourself; a releasing of the darkness within—our own internal struggles—inspiring us to move forward, to evolve.

A crystal symbolizes earth in the South, the physical body, healing, manifesting into physical reality, becoming more active in the world.

A bowl of water symbolizes water in the West, emotions, transforming deep feelings, introspection, clarity, seeing what is hidden.

Incense symbolizes air in the North, wisdom, working on belief systems, learning spiritual truths, aiming toward grace.

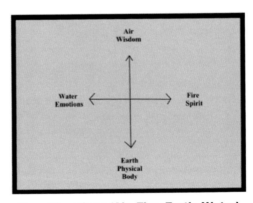

Four Directions (Air, Fire, Earth, Water)

Feel free to add anything that has special meaning to you: a photograph of a loved one, flowers (for their color and beauty), a book that inspires you.

My Altar

If you are lucky enough to have a room of your own, like Virginia Woolf, you can set up a permanent sacred space. I have seen some amazing photos in Pinterest, in which people have built desks in their closets, where, for example, an altar may be added.

Small closet office.

Closet Office in Pinterest

Some friends of mine have even made their sacred space portable, wrapped their altar in a cloth, or in a box, so that they could set up wherever they were. There are travel altars for sale.

An Altar on the Go

Do what you have to do. What is important is finding the objects, connecting to the four elements, and creating a ritual.

Tools

During the next week of **"What Do I Mean By...?" Journaling**, you will need a timer. Find something that does not produce too jarring a ring when it goes off (I use my iTouch which has a lovely sound when it rings). You will also need a set of colored pencils or highlighter pens (I like the *Bic Highlighter* Pens in five colors).

The next step is to find a journal. I love shopping for a new journal. I am particularly fond of the Moleskin blank journal with a black cover, though I've used Composition Books, as well.

Take a moment, reflect, and check in with yourself to be certain that you want to commit to Week 2: **"What Do I Mean By...?" Journaling**. If the answer is yes, go ahead and get started. If you are undecided or hesitant, here is a simple way to start checking in with a deeper aspect of your self. It is called the Body Test, and was adapted from Martha Beck's article in her blog:

26

"Confused about which of your inner voices to trust?"

First of all, stand up, making sure you have some room around you. Take three deep breaths and close your eyes. These are simple ways to ground yourself. Ask a question—it can be a simple one, like "Should I buy a new journal for this week?"—and notice if your body leans forward or backward. If you lean backward, it is a "no." If you lean forward, it is a "yes." Trust the answer. Try this during the week when you feel indecisive, and see what you discover. It is important to verify everything for yourself. Don't just accept what I say, test it out for yourself, and see if it is true for you. It is **you** who matters.

As you may have discovered in the **Two-Pages Journaling**, we all have blind spots. We know these are blind spots because we were unable to see the realization, or belief, for what it was. For example, I may think people are out to get me, and can provide countless examples from my life as "evidence," but after writing example after example in my **Two-Pages Journaling**, I can see that I approach people armed with a certain expectation: they are out to get me. And there it is, my blind spot. Who knows, maybe others think that I'm taking advantage of *them* (A real "Aha!" moment, as my beloved Oprah would say.)?

The best part about a blind spot is that once you recognize it, it is, by definition, no longer a blind spot. Be alert to situations in your life when you feel that this is your truth. You may feel uncomfortable in a given situation, or around a certain person. You have a strong instinct to run away. If you are connected well to yourself—as you will be when you finish reading *The Four Methods of Journal Writing*—then trust your gut. But if you see the same pattern over and over, this is an indication of a blind spot.

Pay attention. It is more likely that the destructive ego part of your self is in charge. This is the time to check in with a trusted, insightful friend, partner, or counselor. Maybe you will learn what all your closest friends already know (and have probably told you many times before, when you were not ready to hear it), or an ally will confirm the reaction you have had, and you will take the necessary action.

My own experience with blind spots has taught me that they sometimes have to come around a few times before I recognize them. It's like a problem that was buried beneath a foundation of unresolved issues and emotions, or like building the house out of good intentions and goals. If it is on shaky ground, it can collapse at any time. I need to see the blind spot with as much clarity as possible, to see all its shadows, how it works, its nuances. In my experience, one cannot do this alone. You need a teacher, counselor, friend, or loved one to point it out to you. Remember, it is called a blind spot because *you* can't see it!

The point of your work this week is to see what lies underneath, to unleash a whole new dimension of your self, one that has the potential for magic. In **"What Do I Mean By...?" Journaling** you have to let what comes up, flow. Follow the thought, that flicker of something in the corner of your consciousness, the synchronicity of an event in your life. You're now spreading your net far to see what you can bring in. It may not be logical. It is unpredictable—but it will be profound.

Purpose, Intention, What to Do

Here we are going to explore a simple, effective way of understanding how you experience life. Take your outline, or mindmap, and prioritize the three - five main issues in your life. These could be health, relationships, finances, home, children, parents, work, sadness, anger, anxiety, sexual issues, addictions, lack of passion, nightmares, worries, spiritual angst, etc. Number them from 1-5, most problematic to least. (It is too much to tackle more than five during the first week.) On Day 1, think of tackling the first major theme, as well as all the sub-categories and issues surrounding it. Often you can follow the thread from one issue to another as they relate to one another.

Sit in front of your altar, light your candle, your incense, and close your eyes. Take a deep breath. Open your eyes and set your timer for thirty minutes. Now write everything you can about your problem (in longhand) in your journal. Stick to this one problem as

28

much as possible. Keep writing without pausing or thinking. When you reach a point where you feel there is nothing more you can say about the problem, add the question, "What do I mean by [?]" and pick from what you have written a key word, phrase, or image that resonates with you, sticks out in the sentence, has energy, or is unusual. Then write that word into the question: "What do I mean by [put the idea, word, image here]?"

Keep writing until there is another pause. Then repeat the same question, and find the next idea, word, image, and ask: "What do I mean by [?]?" until the timer goes off.

On Day 6, read aloud what you have written, preferably to a friend (it can be to yourself). Circle every meaningful word, image, or idea.

On Day 7, go through the words you have marked and highlight them according to category:

Is the word factual (e.g. cancer, depression, mother, IBM, etc.)?

Circle the word(s) in PINK (Fact level)

Is the word emotional (e.g. angry, sad, depressed, excited, jealous; joy, love)?

Circle the word(s) in ORANGE (Emotion level)

Is the word an image (e.g. rainbow, dark clouds, stomping boots; a metaphor, a simile [as if, or like])? Circle the word(s) in YELLOW (Metaphor or Delusion level)

Is the word expressing a sensation (e.g. cracking, tearing, splitting, dense, cloudy, spacey, light, tingling; flying), words about the quality of an action, an object, an animal, a sensation in the body)?

Circle the word(s) in GREEN (Sensation level)

You may find that there are words you've written that seem

29

like nonsense, or that describe the quality of an energy substance (e.g. diving, splashing, tingling, unwrapping; cold, wet, hard, open, etc.) Sometimes you'll find some facts in this list of more abstract words (such as tree, hawk, etc.).

Circle these words in BLUE (Source level)

The experience of this last kind of writing is quite rare, and usually only comes after you've been doing this exercise for a long time (more than five days). Some of you might easily just arrive and be open to Source, naturally "downloading" this kind of journaling. Don't force it. Let it arrive naturally and organically.

When you write spontaneously blue-highlighted words, you will notice that something shifts in you, in the room. Usually time stops. You will feel like you are in endless time, or no time at all. This form of expression in journal writing is a direct connection to Source, and will be experienced in a way that is uniquely your own.

When I take on a homeopathic case, I guide my client to this level of expression. I call it the Source Level, or Level of Energy.

If you are interested in using this method beyond journaling, my trained homeopaths can facilitate and can work with you, using homeopathic remedies to enhance your experience of deep healing. For more information you can visit my website www.InnerHealth.us, or call 617-491-3374. (I have also written a five-part manual on casetaking on this method for homeopaths, *Vital Sensation Correspondence Course Five Part Manual.*)

The Level of Energy is a place where my clients connect to something deep inside them, something that is expressed through a description of a specific substance. This substance can be mineral, plant, animal, or anything in the universe, which can be produced homeopathically.

My experience, and that of my colleagues and students, has demonstrated that a prescription formulated at this level heals deep physical, mental and emotional problems, as well as speeding up spiritual evolution. Clients experience more synchronicities, Aha! moments, miracles, Oneness.

It is possible to access this same Level of Energy through journal writing. The homeopathic remedy supports the process, and because it is a medical modality there are guideposts, which can be used by the practitioner. Through journal writing there is often an unfolding, which happens over a much longer period of time, one that usually addresses primarily the emotional and spiritual realms, rather than the physical symptoms we can better treat with homeopathy.

The words highlighted in pink are at the level of Fact. This is where most of us start out. We name our problem: it is an allergy, or it is a money problem. This naming or labeling of an issue usually closes down our perception of the problem. In this **"What Do I Mean By…?" Journaling**, on the other hand, we're opening up beyond the fact level toward a more comprehensive explanation. For example, when you label your tiredness, anxiety, sadness, as "depression," you may stop observing the unique ways in which these symptoms manifest themselves in you. Eckhart Tolle writes, in *A New Earth: Awakening to Your Life's Purpose,*

"So when you are alert and contemplate a flower, crystal, or bird without naming it mentally, it becomes a window for you into the formless. There is an inner opening, however slight, into the realm of spirit."

I agree hundred percent with Tolle. The same idea applies to any label, be it "depression," "ADD," or anything else. If you forego labeling, you may just experience these states of mind and feeling in a more open way.

The words highlighted in orange are at the level of Emotion. Most people reading this book are likely already in touch with their emotions. We understand another person when they say they are angry or happy, and feel understood ourselves when we can express our emotions and have those feelings accepted. This is often the first stage of healing.

The words highlighted in yellow are at the level of Delusion, not delusion as in "delusional," but as in "metaphorical." These themes—of circumstances and perception—are repeated over and over. (Artists are usually working at this level; they will express an entire idea through a picture, e.g. "(I) felt like I was clawed open," is much more expressive than "I feel vulnerable.") Look at your yellow highlighted words. See if there is a pattern of images, but ignore most of those as un-important, unless they appear repeatedly.

There are major clues here at the level of Delusion, such as the kind of lens through which you may be seeing the world around you. Do you see everyone as your enemy? Do you see yourself as small in the world, or grand? Or what??

The words highlighted in green are at the level of Sensations. Here is where the magic begins! It is here that you cross from left brain to right brain. You are tapping into the morphic field, or Akashic records, or Source. During casetaking as a homeopath, I have often identified when clients shifted from left brain to right brain by the use of a specific expression—I call it a *Vital Sensation*—which signifies a change from an analytic Newtonian perspective to a spiritual Quantum connection.

You can look for this yourself in your green highlighted words. Check to see if there is a word repeated, or one that feels charged, or is expressed in different words of similar meaning. For example, it might be the word *pulsating*. I see this word over and over in my journal writing. This is my *Vital Sensation*.

The next time you work on **"What Do I Mean by...?" Journaling**, put this word or expression in the brackets: "What do I mean by [put your *VITAL SENSATION* (in my case *pulsating*)]?", and start writing. Remember to set your timer for thirty minutes. More often than not, you'll find yourself writing more green-highlighted words, and as you do so, you'll feel the sensations in your body more acutely. The observer in you will feel the transformation in yourself and in the room as you step into Source.

32

Take a deep breath. It is a provocative and life-changing experience to work at this level of Sensation. You are on the brink, about to explore the level of Source. The blue-highlighted words will tumble out of you spontaneously, enriching you, arousing some aspect of yourself that may have lain dormant since you were a child (when you could connect to everything). This is where extraordinary healing, evolution, and enlightenment occur. You do not need to be a yogi to experience this awe-inspiring miracle. Journaling alone can bring you to this space.

Returning to this fifth level, there is still more we are going to be working on over the next weeks, which will focus on journaling as well as on your future memoir.

Let's look over your blue-highlighted (level of Source) words. It might help to write them on a separate piece of paper. See if you can identify what it is that you might be describing. Does it sound like it is something in nature (an animal, a tree, a mineral, the sun—it could be anything, like a magnet)? Ask a friend if they can identify what you have written.

You can explore this further via **"What do I mean by…?" Journaling**. This time write all the "quality words," and leave out the Factual words (you can include the Sensation words) and continue writing. Again, highlight the Source words in blue, and look them over. Can you determine their meaning now? If you can, then go to the Internet, find a picture of the image, and print it out. Carry it with you. Add it to your journal. (If you are still uncertain, then write those blue-highlighted Source words on a card, carry the card with you, and put that in your journal.)

Please email me (newmemoirpress@gmail.com) any observations you experience as you, consciously now, carry with you this image (or the Source words). Enter the Subject Heading "Source," so I will know you have reached this point in your journal writing.

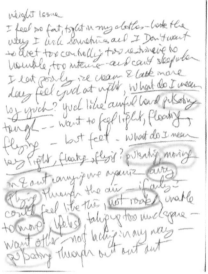

"What Do I Mean by...?" Journaling Pages

Marked with Sensation language, the *Vital Sensation* and Source Words

Vital Sensation: pulsating, moving in & out

Source Words: airy, flying, not rooted, lifeless,

freeing, mushy, springy, white, earth smell, light, moist

I would recommend you stay with the second method of journal writing, **"What Do I Mean by...?" Journaling,** until you reach the Source level. (If you reach this level during the second week or later, then take a break from the inward exploration and go outward, to your interests in the world around you, and connect to your passions in the third method of journal writing, **Inventions Journaling.**)

This second method of journal writing asks us to examine our dis-ease, our health, from the point of view of how many levels of healing we can acknowledge and recognize. There are thousands of books written about the body/mind connection, and here in this journal writing method, you can explore in depth what it means for you.

34

For example, you could be having problems at work; you feel stressed out all the time. You prioritize and decide that this is your main problem. You have noticed that during a particularly stressful day, you experience migraines. Here is a simple body/mind connection—stress at work=migraines.

Through this journal-writing exercise, let's say you notice over and over a word highlighted in green (Sensation level), and the word is *stabbing*. You feel like your co-workers are stabbing you in the back. Your migraines feel like a knife is stabbing you in the forehead. *Stabbing* is a *Vital Sensation*.

As you continue with the exercise, ask yourself "What do I mean by *stabbing*?", and out pours: "crushing, darkness enveloping, tightening, dissolving, cracking, opening, flying, brightness, pink, orange, sweet, "etc. You look over these words and an image appears in your mind: A butterfly. Print out a picture of a butterfly from the Internet, one that resonates with you—the blue butterfly, say—and carry it with you. Put a copy in your journal.

Blue Butterfly

35

Observe the magic that follows. You are offered a job that takes you out of the situation that had been so troubling, and you feel freer, lighter. The migraines stop.

When we turn our attention inward, through journal writing, we become more aware of our body and mind. We observe ourselves more deeply. Maybe it begins with the **Two-Pages Journaling** twenty minutes a day—to **"What Do I Mean By...?" Journaling** thirty minutes a day—to large chunks of the day. Our imagination and our *Vital Sensations* soar.

We become aware of a deeper world of imagination. We are in touch with an overall experience of sensation, a general awareness in our whole being—body and mind. Through journal writing we become aware that all of these levels—facts, emotions, delusions, sensations, Source—are part of us. We experience life physically, mentally, emotionally and spiritually.

The process begins with probing and articulating your suffering in as much detail as possible during the week of **Two-Pages Journaling**. During the week of **"What does it mean by...?" Journaling**, you will discover even deeper layers and connections.

We are tapping into the collective consciousness to identify the exact qualities of a substance we require at the moment. For example, you might find yourself describing a bird that attacks its prey and flies at jet-like speeds. Carrying with you the image of an eagle could change your life.

Test this out for yourself and email me what you discover, at newmemoirpress@gmail.com. I am experiencing goose bumps as I write this request, because I know firsthand the power of this process. I hope you will follow through. Be patient, take your time, and you will find Source and bring it into your consciousness. Let me know what you find out. Truly, I can't wait to hear from you!

Review

1.   Schedule thirty minutes each day for seven days

2.   Create a sacred space. Include a candle, crystal, incense, and a bowl of water

3.   Find a timer, journal, writing pen, and colored pencils (or highlighter pens)

4.   Prioritize the main issues in your life based on your **Two-Pages Journaling** and number them (1-5).

5.   For Days 1 – 5, set the timer for thirty minutes and start writing about the main issues you chose. When there is a pause, write, "What do I mean by [put the idea, word, image here]…? and start writing again until the timer rings.

6.   On Day 6, read aloud your pages, preferably to a friend. Circle every meaningful, powerful word, image, or idea.

7.   On Day 7, go through the marked words and highlight the type of word it is. (Go back and highlight in pink, the factual words; in orange, the emotional words; in yellow, the images or metaphors; in green, the sensation words; in blue, the Source words).

8.   If you find a whole section in blue, try to identify what the words might signify. (If what you come up with seems too abstract, consult a friend.) If you still have no idea, repeat the journal writing, **"What do I mean by** (and fill in those blue highlighted words)**…?"**, and continue to write whatever comes to mind. Repeat this process until it becomes clear what this something could be—in nature, in the universe—and find an image or representation of it on the Internet, print it out and carry it with you. Put a print of the image in your journal. (If it is still too abstract, write the Source [blue-highlighted words] on a card, and carry this with you.) Observe what happens over the next few days, weeks, or months.

9.   If you do not find any blue sections (and it would be unusual to do so in the first week), then see if you have any green-highlighted words that appear often—seeming to jump off the page—and then repeat the **"What do I mean by** (green-highlighted words)**?" Journaling.** Continue to write whatever comes to mind. Over time, you'll find you will be writing more and more Source words, which will lead you to a Source image that can heal and transform you.

10.   If you find there are no green-highlighted words, then continue with the different issues in your life and follow the instructions from the beginning of the **"What Do I Mean By…?" Journaling**.

11.   If you are interested in working with a practitioner who could take you through this process, feel free to email me at newmemoirpress@gmail.com. (Write in the Subject heading "Seeking practitioner.") If you would like more information about Sensation Method Homeopathy, you can read about it at www.innerhealth.us.

12.   Please email me any questions or ideas you have had, or discoveries you have made during this second method of journal writing. I look forward to hearing from you!

13.   I invite you to visit www.new-memoir.co/journal-writing. If you sign up for more information, I will send you more tips, ways to use journaling, information, news of upcoming events, etc.

CHAPTER 3

Inventions Journaling

You must go after your wish. As soon as you start to pursue a dream, your life wakes up and everything has meaning.

— Barbara Sher

Preparation for Week 3

(Or whenever you are ready to move to Journal Writing Method 3)

In Method Three, **Inventions Journaling,** you will need to schedule an hour for the first exercise. The rest of the scheduling will evolve as part of this journal writing method.

Tools

This third method of Journal Writing requires a new journal book. It's time to invest in something special. Your journal should be a minimum size of 7" x 9". (Again, my favorite is the Moleskin Classic Extra Large Soft Cover Plain Notebook Journal [7.5" x 9.75"]). Put together a box of art supplies: colored pencils, watercolors, paintbrushes, tape, colored papers, ribbons, etc. Purchase a 1" spine, three-ring binder and a 1-3 1/2" spine three-ring binder(s), preferably the kind with clear plastic covers. Buy clear plastic sleeves for your three-ring binders, as well as dividers, sticky notes, blank sheets of paper, and index cards. Have your timer ready in case you need it.

Purpose, Intention, What to Do

We are going to take a whole new direction in the third journaling method, **Inventions Journaling**. It is about looking outside ourselves. What are your interests and passions? In Barbara Sher's book, *Refuse to Choose!*, the writer asks us to realize ourselves through what interests us. Sher calls this type of journal writing "your personal version of the Leonardo da Vinci notebooks."

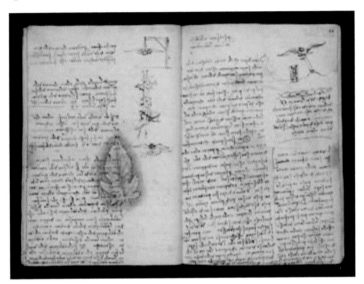

Leonardo da Vinci Journal Page

Pages from Leonardo da Vinci's *Codex on the Flight of Birds* (ca. 1490-1505, pen and brown ink on 18 bound sheets, 213 x 153 mm, Ms. Varia 95). From the Collection of the Biblioteca Reale, Turin. Photographs by Fabrizio Fenucci

You will use this journal-writing method to capture your ideas, your private thoughts, "what ifs," your interests, your creative thoughts, your visions.

...the very act of considering your explorations worth keeping track of begins to change everything you ever thought about yourself.

— Barbara Sher, *Refuse to Choose!*

40

"Where does your mind really want to go?" Sher asks, and by answering this question you will start to value your ideas and become fascinated with anything new, without all the pressure of their becoming a "To-Do List." You are free to plan without commitment, when you have the inspiration, no strings attached. You'll be the sole inventor of your life through the **Inventions Journaling** process.

Day 1

Pick an idea that interests you. It could be anything, the memoir you plan to write, a film you want to make, an outfit you want to wear, a recipe you'd like to prepare, a project you'd like to realize at work—something that is current and exciting would be ideal.

In the upper left corner of the left side of the page, put the date, and give your idea a title (centered at the top of the left side of the page). Now let yourself go!

1. Write about the idea in your journal

Inventions Journaling Page

2. Mindmap the idea in your journal: draw a circle and put the title inside the circle. Draw smaller circles with other related ideas, and then branch out from there.

3. Draw simple images, stick figures, etc.

4. Cut out images from magazines, or the Internet, that relate to your idea and tape them into your book.

5. If your mind goes off on a tangent, or if something unrelated to the idea comes to mind, draw an arrow in the upper right corner. Turn the page, date the left hand corner, and write the title of the new idea at top of the next page in the same way as before. Write about this tangent idea for no more than 10 minutes (set your timer), and then go back to the main idea of the day, knowing that the tangent idea is available for another **Inventions Journaling** session. (You can't lose the tangent idea now!).

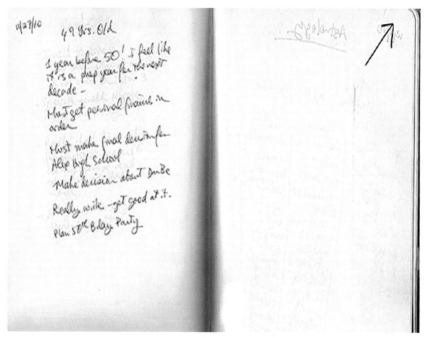

Inventions Journaling Tangent Page

6. Write a complete description of your idea in as much detail as possible. Imagine it fully, as if it already exists, and write from this perspective.

You are the creator with **Inventions Journaling**. It's a chance to observe your creative mind.

Take out your calendar and schedule Day 2 at a time when you can make a one-hour date with yourself for **Inventions Journaling**. (Be sure to write it in your calendar.) If someone wants to schedule something during that hour, you can say you have a prior engagement. Few people will question this response.

Day 2

Start on a new page, date the upper left corner, and entitle it "Your Map." Look around your home, your office, your hard copy files, your computer desktop, and draw or list any unfinished projects.

Inventions Journaling Mindmap Page

The idea is to re-capture all the interests you've had in the past. (The idea is not to beat yourself up for what is as yet unfinished.). It's a way to get a fix on what was important to you in the past, and what may still be important in the present so you can generate new opportunities and move forward with less resistance, more fun.

Take out your calendar and schedule Day 3 at a time when you can make a one-hour date with yourself for **Inventions Journaling**.

Day 3

Repeat what you did on Day 1 on a new page (blank left and right pages). Write the date on the upper left corner and give the idea a name. Just go for it! Observe how you loosen up, get fired up with this new idea. Use your colored pencils and markers to add images. Describe your ideas in detail.

Again, if you have a tangent idea, draw an arrow in the upper right corner, turn the page, date it, title it, and write about the new idea for ten minutes. Then go back to the original idea on the previous page.

Take out your calendar and schedule Day 4 at a time when you can make a one-hour date with yourself for the next **Inventions Journaling** session.

Day 4

On a fresh page, write the date in the upper left corner, and label it "My Accomplishments and Experiences." Write everything you can remember—dressing up as a robot for Halloween, getting married, passing the bar exam, writing a poem, painting a self-portrait—including projects that failed or were never finished. (For example: the book you planned to write, but didn't.)

Set your timer for five minutes and start. Write down everything that you can think of.

It's all right to acknowledge your failures as well as your successes. They both have value, and have led you to where you are now, and where you are heading.

Look over your list and consider which activities gave you a charge, when you felt you were *in the zone*. Competent, you loved the work, the project, the idea. Circle those accomplishments and experiences even if in the end they failed or were never finished.

Make a short list of the five top projects that gave you this zing in life.

Start on a fresh page, date the left upper corner, and write the title, "What I want to Accomplish." Set your timer for twenty minutes and write. Pay close attention to the sensations in your body. Write down not just anything that pops into your head, but what makes you tingle, breathe deeply.

Look over your list, item by item, and do the body test. If you lean forward, number it as #1, #2, etc. (Leave the item out if you leaned backward when that particular idea was raised.) Trust your body instincts in this exercise.

If you have time, you can make a list of those things you would never want to do. This list could be an interesting source as you begin to say no to things, allowing more time for what you truly want to do.

Take out your calendar and schedule Day 5 at a time when you can make a one-hour date with yourself for **Inventions Journaling**. Bring your binders, and be sure to have access to a copying machine.

Day 5

Take your 1", three-ring binder and make a list of the projects you numbered. Put the paper inside one of the plastic sleeves so it will be easy to update and preserve. Stick this in the front of the binder. Label your three-ring binder "INVENTIONS," or some other title that makes you sing.

Create a divider for each item on your list and put these in your binder. Next to the divider, add a plastic sleeve in which to collect any ideas you write on index cards, or any print-outs from the computer, file names/folders for future reference, etc.

Photocopy any of the pages related to one of your inventions from this journal and stick it in the appropriate plastic sleeve. File it in the 1" binder. If it turns out that the plastic sleeve is full, take one of the 1/2" three-ring binders, label it with the name of this project, and start adding all your ideas to this binder. (You can also keep a folder on the computer labeled with the name of the project and add your ideas there). It is important to have one actual binder with a log of all the projects (make a note, if you have a computer file on the paper log).

If you have time available, pick one of the projects and continue adding to it. You can research on the Internet, brainstorm, plan, or write. All of these ideas will be filed in your three-ring binders and/or in your computer. **Inventions Journaling** is meant to be fun. Allow the process to unfold. Some projects will be filed only in your journal, others may make it to the 1" binder. Some will expand to the 1/2" binder, and others will blossom into full-blown projects.

Start to carry a few index cards and post-its with you to jot down ideas as they come. Write one idea on one index card, date it, and add the title of the project. If you see an interesting fact, quote, or reference, write it on the post-it to be added to **Inventions Journaling,** or in one of the binders. You'll be collecting all the loose ideas, leads, and pieces of information. At the end of the day, put everything in a clear plastic sleeve for filing in your binders during your next **Inventions Journaling** session.

Take out your calendar and schedule Day 6 at a time when you can make a one-hour date with yourself for **Inventions Journaling**.

Day 6

File your index cards and post-its from the week before in your **Inventions Journaling** or in your binders.

Is writing a memoir on your list of projects? If not, is it in your Invention Journal? If you answered yes, then jump ahead to Day 7 (below). If not, then you may have other major projects that you must do first. This is totally all right. Pick one that grabs you, and follow up on it during your hour. Or start on something new, something that you feel just must be explored immediately. There is no right or wrong here.

Perhaps my question has reminded you of the memoir you want to write. Great! Start with your Inventions Journal, date the left hand corner, write "Memoir" at the top of the page, and begin. Add any ideas, memories, scenes, thoughts, overviews—anything that comes to mind. Tape in pictures, photos, or mementoes. Keep adding until your time runs out.

Take out your calendar and schedule Day 7 at a time when you can make a one-hour date with yourself for **Inventions Journaling**.

Day 7

If you have been working on your memoir, continue where you left off. Keep brainstorming. Write down any memories, research anything that is relevant. Keep things open, at this stage.

If some other project has you excited, then continue where you left off on that project. If you are ready to explore more ideas, then add to your Inventions Journal (as in Day 1).

From now on, use these tools as you feel inspired. You may find that you stay mostly with the Inventions Journal, or that one project is expanding itself into multiple binders as it takes on a life of its own. Let new ideas take their course, either toward completion, or as signposts of your interests in that moment. Everything is good here. No judgment.

This way of recording all your ideas (and filing them as efficiently as possible) frees up the brain and forces you to pay attention to your mind, observing how it works, what attracts you to things, what repels you.

The **Inventions Journaling** method is based on several ideas taken from Barbara Sher's book, *Refuse to Choose!*. (The book goes into much greater depth than I do here. This topic may also be of special interest for those with ADD tendencies.) I highly recommend that you buy her book and see what else she has to say on the subject.

There will be so many projects inspired by this third method of journal writing. Passion will return to your life, and you'll be able to navigate new territory (especially if you have been feeling scattered because of too many ideas, or overwhelmed as to how to get started). Who knows, you may just be the inventor of the next widget that everyone is waiting for!

Remember to take yourself seriously. You are an inventor, and your ideas matter. It is so important to acknowledge how we manifest in our lives. When you follow these three methods of journal writing, in order, you will be working from the inside out, discovering aspects of yourself, which will nourish all of you. I can't wait to see who you are becoming, and in what ways you will contribute and serve humanity.

Review

1. Pick up the following supplies:

- a new blank journal, at least 7" x 9" (e.g. the Moleskin Extra Large Soft Cover Plain Notebook Journal)

- put together a box of art supplies: colored pencils, paint brushes, water colors, tape, colored paper, ribbons, etc.

- a timer

- one 1" spine, three-ring binder

- 1-3 ½" spine, three-ring binders

- clear plastic sleeves

- dividers

- sticky notes (Post-its)

- index cards

- blank paper

2. Schedule 1 hr. sessions

3. Day 1, pick an idea and write about it in your Invention Journal

4. Day 2, make an inventory of all your unfinished projects

5. Day 3, repeat Day 1

6. Day 4:

- Make a list of all your accomplishments and experiences

- Chose the five top projects in your life

- Write out what you want to accomplish now

- Body test each new project, and note in a numbered list

the projects that test positive

7. Day 5:

   - Make a log of all the numbered projects you identified, and file them in the 1" binder

   - Create dividers for each project that was numbered

   - Photocopy any **Inventions Journaling** pages related to the numbered projects, and insert the copies into clear plastic sleeves. File them in the 1- 3 ½" binders

   - Carry index cards and post-its with you for writing down any quotes or references, or any ideas, you may have. File them in a clear plastic sleeve

8. Day 6, commit to your memoir project, or another project that is calling you—follow your gut here—and work on it. If you are unsure, use the Body Test and follow through with the answers you get. (If you feel strongly that you want to contradict the Body Test, this is an opportunity to see if that reaction is, in fact, a blind spot. Ask a trusted friend, family member, or counselor to help you sort out why your Body Test indicates one answer, but you feel impelled to ignore it. Explore the possibility that there is an aspect of your self that may want to sabotage your efforts; it could also be that some other understanding lies behind this contradiction. Seek to go deep to resolve this conflict within yourself.)

9. Day 7, repeat Day 6

CHAPTER 4

Autobiography Journaling

> *There is always one moment in childhood when the door opens and lets the future in.*

— Graham Greene, *The Power and the Glory*

Preparation for Week 4

(Or whenever you are ready to move to Journal Writing Method 4)

Y ou will need large blocks of time (at least one hour, though two to four hours would be better, if you can schedule it) for this method. Once again choose a sacred space in which to write, preferably one with your altar in place, so that you can bring in the four elements, Source, and power to your practice. You will be working from the inside out, this time through the window of memory.

Your altar should have a candle in order to invite fire energy; incense to carry air energy; a crystal to anchor earth energy; and water to help the flow of water energy.

Tools

You will need:

- a new journal. (Try to find one that has dividers. Some spiral notebooks have five subject dividers)

- your favorite pen or pencil

- a set of colored pencils or highlighter pens

- a timer

- Epsom Salts and lavender essential oil

Purpose, Intention, What to Do

The **Autobiography Journal** is a way to map your life (so far) in five-year blocks. Nancy shared this method with me the year before my fiftieth birthday. You do not have to have reached the age of fifty to reap the benefits; you can engage in this type of journaling at any age.

The roots of reflection went deep into my core so that a channel opened—one that I could tap into authentically, magically. This channel kindled in me the desire to write my memoir. You may already have discovered inspiration via the **Inventions Journaling**, but for me it did not come until after learning this fourth method, **Autobiography Journaling**. The magic worked slowly, almost as an afterthought to my exploration of self, until it culminated in my memoir, which was completed in ten months.

I can't predict what this experience will be like for you, but since you are reading this book, *Four Methods of Journal Writing: Self-development Through Memoir*—the subject must have resonated somehow. Here you are on the edge of the cliff. Now it is time to jump.

Write this journal based on your memories. (Note: This is not the time to check with family and friends as to how their memories jibe with yours. Keep this remembering to yourself, for now. You will have plenty of time to check your facts, find out what may really have happened, etc. when you are writing your memoir.) With **Autobiography Journaling,** you will want to write the memories in brush strokes, not in full scenes. Be as specific as possible: the image, the texture, the impressions, the emotions, the dialogues, dreams, sensations, colors, patterns—any details you can remember. Don't write every aspect (there'll be plenty of room for that in your actual memoir), just the memories that come to you in the moment

Autobiography Journaling Page

Write out five-year blocks of your life in your journal:

1-5 years	36-40 years	71-75 years
6-10 years	41-45 years	76-80 years
11-15 years	46-50 years	81-85 years
16-20 years	51-55 years	86-90 years
21-25 years	56-60 years	91-95 years
26-30 years	61-65 years	96-100 years
31-35 years	66-70 years	

..and beyond (if you a centenarian and reading this book, I stand in awe of you!).

Write what you can remember for each of the five-year blocks in a separate section of your journal. (It took me an hour for my first ten years, and then about an hour for each five-year block after that.) Plan accordingly, so you won't feel rushed. Do what you can with the time you have, but try not to stop in the middle of a five-year block. Better to end early than to have to stop in the middle.

This **Autobiography Journal** could be completed in one weekend. You can engage in this practice alone, in your sacred space, but it's also a wonderful project to do with friends. When you set up your altar, invite everyone to contribute to the sacred space so that everyone's gifts are represented.

You may find your energy dipping, or you may become overly excited, and then feel drained. This is normal. A wide range of emotions and energy levels is to be expected.

Remember to start each five-year block in a new section of your journal. You can skip five to ten pages and then start the next five-year block, if you don't have dividers (or enough dividers).

Depending on your scheduling of **Autobiography Journaling**, there may be a natural time to pause. Be sure to take a break before you start the next step.

Take your colored pencils or highlighters and go through all of your writing:

- highlight in pink: pain, suffering and bad feelings

- highlight in orange: fear

- highlight in blue: pleasure and good feelings

- highlight in yellow: people (include pets in this category)

-        highlight in green: places

-        use an asterix (*) for any important turning points in your life

-        draw a squiggly line under any *related* memories (a memory that was told you, not directly experienced or remembered by you)

Use the left side of the blank page. Draw four quadrants: two lines, a vertical line through the center of the page, and a vertical line across the page. Write the names of all the people in the upper left. Write all the locations in the upper right. Write all the painful points in the lower left. Write all the positive points in the lower right.

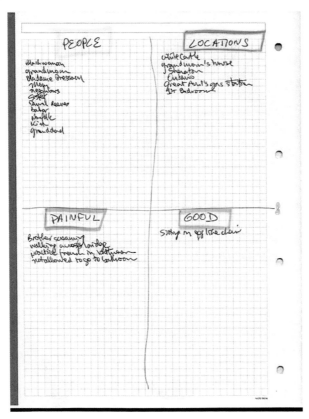

Autobiography Journaling Page of Four Quadrants

Use the right side of the blank page. Draw a horizontal line across the page, and mark off the five-year blocks. Label each with the year in which the turning point occurred.

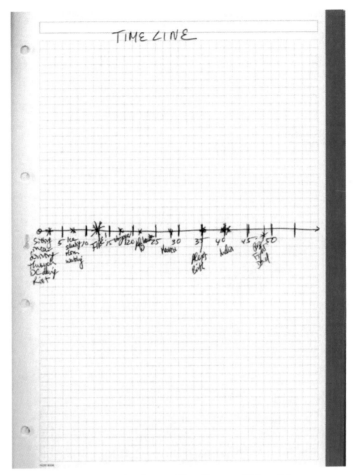

Autobiography Journaling Page of Time Line

Take a break. If you are part of a group, this is time to share any "Aha!" moments, anything significant that came up for you, or any thoughts about your experience of **Autobiography Journaling**. If you are doing this alone, feel free to write your feelings in general for each stage, each turning point, as well as any observations, patterns, or anything new that is revealed.

The Four Quadrant page and the Time Line are like a snapshot of your life to date. Observe your physical reactions to the pages—any sensations, thoughts. Let them pass. Don't try to change them. Don't make plans for them, just observe them as they are.

When you have completed the **Autobiography Journal** it is important to detox. I would recommend taking a hot bath, pouring in 2 to 4 cups of Epsom Salts, adding lavender essential oil, and soaking for at least twenty minutes. Your body will need a release after this experience, and this is a gentle way in which to provide that.

You will experience a strong, conscious awareness, and you will want to share this with loved ones. Take your time. Enjoy the positive memories and let go of the negative ones. At this stage, after **Autobiography Journaling**, there will be more of a sense of detachment from your memories. You'll see the events and the memories as if they had happened to a third person.

If you have the sense of an unconscious aspect simmering under the surface, then you need to pay attention to this feeling. If there are some leftover issues from **Autobiography Journaling**, then go back to **Two-Pages Journaling**, and write—every morning for twenty minutes—whatever comes to mind. You may wind up writing about a feeling you have had, or you may not. Trust that whatever you write now is meant to leave your subconscious and free you. Let this be your practice until you feel complete from the experience. Trust in the amount of time you need. (If you are unsure, use the Body Test to check when it is time for you to move on to the final step: **Memoir Writing**.)

Review

1. Pick up the following supplies:

- new blank journal, one with dividers

- five colored pencils or highlighter pens

- favorite pen

2.   Schedule your **Autobiography Journaling** sessions (invite friends to join you, if that feels right)

3.   Write your memories in five-year blocks (taking a break after each block, and starting each one in a new section of the journal)

4.   Read through your text and mark it:

- highlight in pink: pain, suffering and bad feelings

- highlight in orange: fear

- highlight in blue: pleasure and good feelings

- highlight in yellow: people (include pets in this category)

- highlight in green: places

- use an asterix (*) for any important turning points in your life

- draw a squiggly line under any *related* memories (a memory that was told you, not directly experienced or remembered by you).

5.   Map the memories in four quadrants, draw vertical and horizontal lines on the left page. Write people's names in the upper left quadrant. Write the locations in the upper right quadrant, the painful points in the lower left quadrant, and, in the lower right

quadrant, all the positive points.

6.   On the right side of a blank page, draw a horizontal line. Mark five-year blocks and label and date the important turning points you identified.

7.   Review your work. Summarize any themes. Share with friends and/or write your feelings, your "Aha!" moments—anything that stands out for you.

8.   Observe the impressions as they occur. Do not act on any of them at this time, just watch them pass through you.

9.   After you have completed the final step of the **Autobiography Journaling,** take a hot bath with Epsom Salts and essential oils.

10.   You may want to follow up this fourth and final Journal Writing method with **Two-Pages Journaling** every morning. This time, however, write whatever comes to mind, not necessarily the negative situations in your life. Let the words flow freely, until you feel complete with the experience.

CHAPTER 5

Writing Your Memoir

Write about small, self-contained incidents that are still vivid in your memory. If you remember them, it's because they contain a larger truth that your readers will recognize in their own lives. Think small and you'll wind up finding the big themes in your family saga.

— William Knowlton Zinsser

I think all of us have a yearning to tell our story. It may happen now, or later. Trust where you are. You've accomplished something profound via *The Four Methods of Journal Writing,* and many healing changes are in process. The memoir is a full integration of what you've been through, and an acknowledgement of your life. It holds the potential to be read by a large audience, a validation of your life experience.

I started my memoir after finishing the **Autobiography Journal**. I felt a deep need to write. I wasn't sure if I would write a memoir, or another sort of book. I went back to **Two-Pages Journaling**, which grew to "Five Pages Journaling." I no longer wrote only about what was troubling me in the present, but also memories, stories I had told many times to friends and loved ones, and even theories I had about life. Every morning I woke up and wrote for an hour and a half.

My friend, Nancy, and I made a date to contact each other at 6:00 a.m. every day. I would call her at her home in Brooklyn and listen to her sleepy voice saying "I will call you later." This was our code to begin writing.

I wrote for several months (Nothing I was willing to share with others. I was private, like the pregnant mother keeping her secret until the baby shows). The new year arrived, and I kept writing—during the early hours, in the dark—stopping only when the sun rose on the horizon. The writing affected my days. It felt as if I had run a marathon every morning. I was not as clear or present after the writing sessions. But I kept at it.

Soon I felt inspired to start work on my memoir. I wrote the first two pages—a summary of my twenties in two pages. I showed it to Nancy, who said it needed to be expanded. Clearly, if ten years could be outlined in two pages, then the memoir could easily grow to many more pages.

Nancy and I met in New York at the end of January. We gave a title to the potential memoir, a working title based on some of the ideas and issues contained in its pages. Nancy and I brainstormed all the major ideas, stories, themes. She took notes. The memories and ideas were arranged in chronological order, decade by decade, organized by the communities in which I lived at the time: first, the Penington Friends House, a Quaker living community in Manhattan; then Auroville, a Spiritual community in South East India; and, finally, Cornerstone Cohousing Community, where I live now in Cambridge, MA. When we finished the outline, it looked as if there was enough material for four books altogether!

Nancy suggested that I read some published memoirs. I've always been a reader, taking on at least one book a week for most of my life, but up until this point I had only read books about health, homeopathy, spirituality, self-help, and business. Not much fiction, poetry, or memoir.

I immersed myself in memoir, among them *The Liar's Club*, by Mary Karr, *I know Why the Caged Bird Sings,* by Maya Angelou, Jill Conway's *The Road from Coorain*, Martha Beck's *Leaving the Saints: How I lost the Mormons and Found My Faith,* and Patricia Hampl's *I Could Tell You Stories: Sojourns in the Land of Memory.*

61

Some Favorite Memoirs (courtesy Pinterest)

I also read books on writing memoirs, such as *Writing Life Stories: How to Make Memories Into Memoirs, Ideas Into Essays, and Life Into Literature*, by Bill Roorbach, *The Situation and the Story: The Art of Personal Narrative*, by Vivian Gornick, and many other books on the subject of craft. I found all these wonderful books in the library—a new discovery! (The books I had read in the past rarely were available there. And, anyway, I read most books as soon as they appeared in the bookstore.)

Nancy and I continued our 6:00 a.m. writing sessions. By February I was following my outline, writing with this anchor—one idea, one story—it was hard, slow, only five hundred words a day. It was exhausting, but also exhilarating.

I went to bed early, entering a cocoon stage of life. I felt drawn to my morning memoir writing, fitting it in no matter what. I stopped socializing, and dropped out of social media. I kept my life simple, putting myself on an austerity program to make my money last. I vowed to take as few homeopathic clients as possible and to stop teaching full time.

My day became more and more about the writing, the reading, and the study of writing. A month later, my first chapter was finished. Fifteen pages about my journey to Afghanistan after the Soviet invasion. Personal, daring, fresh material. I felt raw, naked.

My husband, George, read it. He liked it! I was happy with his response, but knew I had to show it to someone who, unlike my husband, was *not* my biggest fan. Nancy read it next and she liked it, too. (And she can be critical. It is not in her nature to offer praise unless it's due.) Two more friends (both editors) gave it the *thumbs up*. I was finally feeling secure in the knowledge that the first chapter had some merit; a true first draft, for sure, but one that seemed to have potential.

I kept writing daily, 6:00 a.m. to 8:00 a.m. I could write 1,000 words a day now. Like a runner in training, the muscle gets stronger, and the work becomes easier. I could feel myself surrender to the process. Memories surfaced that I hadn't thought of in years. They arrived in the form of smells, sounds, textures, sights. I wrote what I felt, heard, and saw. Scenes from my past appeared, with characters, dialogue, and locations. I breathed through the process step by step, uncovering patterns, reviewing where one event connected to another, layering scenes, summaries and narration. I used the Internet to fact check, read my journals to insure the accuracy of my memory, and asked some family members what they remembered.

I was gradually becoming a writer. I signed up for my first writers' workshop, a one-day event at Grub Street, in Boston. I wanted to step out of my inner fan club and share my work with fellow writers under the guidance of a teacher. I picked the first three pages of the first chapter on Afghanistan to read. As I read, I could feel the titillating shock of an audience enraptured by the words I had written. The encouragement of the class spurred me on.

My world stayed small while I wrote: family life, a few clients and students, my spiritual practice, the co-housing community in which I lived, a few friends. Now I was three chapters in—over hundred pages! I signed up for a weekly writing group, and had the first chapter workshopped. The students and teacher read the piece, line by line, suggesting ways in which to improve it.

I signed up for another writing group, and workshopped another chapter, stepping further into the world of writers and writing. The chapters started to build momentum, like the flywheel. It required very little effort for me to produce 2,000 words daily. Soon the first draft was written: 197 pages. I had done it!

This journey to memoir writing proved to be an opportunity to grow, to evolve, and to integrate aspects of my life—from childhood, adolescence, young adulthood, middle age, to maturity. My self was exposed, deepened, by this experience, this awakening, this journey to uncover memories, inner beliefs, and philosophies that I needed to share.

As I look back over the past ten months—which began with writing whatever came to mind, and developed into the more structured memoir writing—I am amazed. It has been a transformative experience to become a writer, a creator, to collect memories and thoughts in a form that can potentially entertain others, teach others, inspire others.

When I was in my twenties I produced a national public television series about women's lives called "Women in Limbo Presents." In a very public forum I talked about my weight issues, my difficult mother, my ambitions, and now twenty years later I had revisited that time in my life, but this time with the wisdom of years. It was a most authentic, validating experience.

My favorite memoirs are like best friends. I start reading and if something clicks right away, then I can easily discover its essence: what makes me laugh, cry, nod "yes, yes!" (or "no, no!"), or think, "I don't want that to happen to you, or anyone else, and yet… you survived!" What's more, I know that you (the writer) are stronger for having told your story, for sharing publicly your pains, your joys, your love.

I cannot teach you how to write a memoir in the same way that I gave you daily tasks around journal writing, but I can encourage you to try it, to tell your story and share it for all to read. I certainly want to read your story, and others will, too. I want to step into your life in this most intimate of ways, to find myself in the place where your wisdom shines, where you share what matters most to you. It would be an honor to be a part of your life in this way. Vicariously—on my Kindle, or reading on my couch—I might be able to enter the world of your memories.

The artist is the gift-giver in our culture, and the memoir writer has profound gifts to share. I urge you to write your memoir, and, when it is published, be sure to send me an autographed copy.

Review:

1.   Schedule your memoir writing for five days a week

2.   Plan to write at least 500 words each writing session

3.   Read memoirs and books about the craft of writing

4.   Brainstorm all your memories, stories, and ideas and organize the material into an outline

5.   Write at least 500 words each day, based on one of your outline points

6.   When you are ready, share a chapter with a literary friend, a writing group, a writing workshop, a class (at this stage in the process hold your baby close, and be careful who you share it with).

7.   Keep going—write your memoir

8.   You do not have to write your memoir alone, without any professional help. Find an editor to guide you. Remember your blind spot (you may need to listen to the feedback you receive). Use the Body Test to check if an editor (or the critic, if you wish to argue with the advice) is the right one for you.

9.   Write several drafts of your memoir. The first draft is the spewing out of everything within you. Each draft is a refinement. You are creating art, so take your time. But do complete the project.

10.   Publish your memoir (either self, small press, or major publishing house). Let the public read about your life!

POSTCRIPT

I wrote *The Four Methods of Journal Writing: Self-Transformation through Memoir* while waiting for my editor to review the manuscript of my memoir. I was so used to writing every day, I could not sit still without it, so set to work on this book. I had written 4,000 words by noon! I suddenly realized that I was going to write an entire book in one day. At midnight, I was done. I had written 12,000 words.

Melissa Burch after Writing
The Four Methods of Journal Writing:
Self-Transformation through Memoir
in one day

RESOURCES

1. Beck, Martha. *The Four-Day Win: End Your Diet War and Achieve Thinner Peace.* New York: Rodale, Inc., 2007.

2. Cameron, Julia. *The Artist's Way.* New York: Tarcher/Putnam, 1992.

3. Collins, Jim. *Good to Great: Why Some Companies Make the Leap…and Others Don't.* New York: Harper Collins Publishers Inc., 2001.

4. Covey, Stephen R. *The 7 Habits of Highly Effective People.* New York: Free Press, 1989.

5. Ford, Debbie. The *Dark Side of the Light Chasers: Reclaiming Your Power, Creativity, Brilliance, and Dreams.* New York: Riverhead Books, 1998.

6. Gornick, Vivian. *The Situation and the Story: The Art of Personal Narrative.* New York: Farrar, Straus and Giroux, 2001.

7. Roorbach, Bill. *Writing Life Stories: How to Make Memories Into Memoirs, Ideas Into Essays, and Life Into Literature.* Cincinnati: F+W Publications, Inc., 2008.

8. Sher, Barbara. *Refuse to Choose!* Stuttgart: Holtzbrinck Publishers, 2006.

9. Tolle, Eckhart. *A New Earth – Awakening to Your Life's Purpose.* New York: Penguin Group, 2005.

10. Woolf, Virginia. *A Room of One's Own.* Orlando: Harcourt, Inc., 1929.

ACKNOWLEDGMENTS

My deepest appreciation goes to my husband who keeps cheering me on when I have a new idea, even if it is to write a book in one day. The completion of this book took much longer and without George's support you would not be reading it. Thank you to my editor Sue Halliday, who made sure the grammar, punctuation and spelling were professional. Susana Aikin is my inspiration to become a writer and a best friend when the road gets a bit challenging.

Made in the USA
San Bernardino, CA
22 August 2014